Go to the Ant

A simple but effective guide for day to day money management

Isaac N. P. Carter

MINISTRY IN ART PUBLISHING

communicating excellence

Ministry In Art Publishing Ltd
email admin@ministryinart.com
www.miapublishing.com

This publication is designed to provide accurate and
authoritative information in regard to the subject matter
covered. It is sold with understanding that the publisher is not
engaged in rendering legal, accounting, or other professional
service. If legal advice or other expert assistance is required,
the services of a competent professional
should be sought.

ISBN: 978-1-907402-01-2

Illustrations by Natasha Williams
Cover design by Allan Sealy
(www.miadesign.com)

CONTENTS

ACKNOWLEDGEMENTS

Thanks to:

My late, Father Isaac Newton Carter (Snr), and my Mother Enid Carter, who always encouraged me never to settle but to reach for the stars.

To Wayne Malcolm, probably the best life coach and motivator I know, who inspired me to believe that I could do this.

To Len Allen, a great mentor and a great mate.

To Elisabeth (Chidi), Bibiana, Maureen and Anthony (my super support group) who greatly assisted me in refining the basic draft of this book until it began to take shape as something worthy of publication.

To my Wife Pauline Carter who encouraged me for years to take responsibility for and manage my finances, and my two beautiful children, Isaac and Natalie.

www.gototheant.co.uk

Go to the Ant thou sluggard consider her ways,
which having no guide, overseer or ruler provideth
her meat in the summer and gathereth her food in
the harvest for the winter:

Proverb

FOREWORD

The Ant

As the Proverb states have you ever stopped to consider the Ant? Industrious, organised, always thinking about and preparing for the future, so there will be enough, so there will be no lack either in good or bad times.

In the economy of the Ant there is no recession, no meltdown, no boom bust cycle; it is never caught short. Wouldn't it be great if we, as humans, could learn from the Ant with regards to our finances; to plan, strategize and prepare for the future?

Just think about the way the Ant goes about its business:

*   Ants don't do credit

*   Ants don't borrow

*   Ants organize hunt and store in the good times so they are ready for the bad

*   Ants never run out of resources

*   Ants always have enough

The Ant is the essence of organization; every mission is planned with strategic emphasis and military precision with clear aims and objectives, whether it is the construction of a colony, the collection of food or the destruction of an enemy. The Ant is focused and perseveres; it overcomes obstacles, is never defeated and never gives up.

This is the approach you have to adopt towards the structuring of your financial affairs.

www.gototheant.co.uk

INTRODUCTION

As this book goes to press we are in the middle of a world- wide economic meltdown; a crisis which is being termed the "credit crunch". As this is not an economics book we need not go into specific details; what is clear however is that the major financial institutions throughout the western world have over extended themselves in credit and bad debt thereby leading to a loss of economic confidence in the world's major economies. This in turn has led to a down turn which has affected the lives of individuals from the top to the bottom of the social scale throughout this country and indeed the world.

The most significant effects of the "credit crunch" have been felt in the following sectors of the financial industry:

1. Banks, stung by over extending themselves and incurring massive losses are now refusing to extend credit facilities to each other and businesses.

2. The resulting loss of trust and confidence has led to a meltdown of the major stock markets in the world including London, Wall Street, Tokyo, and Berlin.

3. Major Financial Institutions have been sent to the wall and some have actually gone under; Lehman Brothers, Freddie Mac, Fanny Mae, HBOS, and Goldman Sachs.

However, nowhere has the effects of the above crisis been felt more acutely than on the average man and woman on the street. Rising fuel bills, petrol and food prices, rising unemployment, falling property prices, increased repossessions, defaulting commercial and residential loans, increasing IVF arrangements and personal bankruptcies.

Frightening isn't it? And what makes the current situation even worse is the fact that we have just come out of a period of supposedly record financial prosperity, unrivalled economic growth financed by massive growth in property, boom in consumer spending, all fuelled by low interest and freely available credit.

So what happened? How did it go so wrong so quickly? Why didn't we spot it? Surely this was not foreseeable, or was it?

Although this book does not claim to be degree level economics it can be clearly stated that the history of the British, European and indeed all the World's major economies can be understood on a simple gravitational principle "what goes up will come down", or in more familiar economic terminology, after every boom usually comes a bust or a crash.

Yes, there are unique factors in this particular crash, however in simple terms given the same economic and financial patterns and indicators you will always get the same results. You would think that if we knew what was coming we would prepare, wouldn't you?

I hear you saying what does this have to do with the Ant?

As I said above, the Ant is never caught short it's always preparing, always storing, always building, so whatever the times, good or bad it has provision; in other words, the Ant is future focused.

In this book we will learn how to be like the Ant when it comes to managing our own finances, how to take control, get organised, make our money work for us, eliminate debt and be ready financially for whatever comes next!!!

In other words we want to be financially intelligent! Come; let's go learn from the Ant!!!!

How to get the Most out of this Book

This is a practical book or what you might call a "how to" book so we can walk through it together, step by step, ticking off each point and going through each stage until we reach our final destination together.

The best way to get the most out of this book is as follows:

- **Take your time:** Because this book is not the size of "War and Peace" there might be a tendency to try and read it all in one day; please don't! Read each chapter thoroughly, make notes and then follow any instructions set out in the chapter before moving on.

- At the end of each chapter there are a number of steps you are required to take before you move on. **Follow each step carefully before moving on**; this way you will see the actual progress in the management of your finances.

- Use this book as a working tool and as it helps you, use it to help your partner, your children (it's never too early to start managing your finances) and your friends; better still, recommend they purchase the book.

www.gototheant.co.uk

*Did you know that in some Ant colonies there are
up to 70,000 Ants all with specific roles,
duties which they carry out every day?*

CHAPTER 1

TAKING STOCK

One of the first rules of warfare is to know your enemy, and believe me taking control of your finances is a battle when you have let things drift for a while. Mess only brings stress and therefore before we can organize our finances we have to get ourselves organised.

So, the first thing you need to do is ascertain exactly what position you are in, be it good, bad or really bad! This is not going to be painless; sometimes the worst part of overcoming any illness or problem is facing up to the enormity of the diagnosis. This is where you take a long hard look at your finances, the good, bad and ugly! But, on the positive side, once you make a decision to sort things out, you are on your way.

The first step is to examine your financial position by doing a number of taking stock exercises, or in other words carrying out your own financial audit.

Income and Expenditure

Firstly, you need to examine your income and expenditure. This should be a fairly basic exercise; your income is money coming to you and an expense is money you are spending, or more significantly money going away from you.

Examples of income:

Salary,
Child Benefit
Rental income (investment property),
Investment income (interest, dividends),
Pension

Examples of expenditure would include:

Rent/mortgage,
Credit cards,
Loans,
Utility bills,
Daily living expenses;

Assets and Liabilities

Secondly, you need to carry out an asset and liabilities audit. This is done by making a list of all your assets and liabilities. Put simply, an asset is something of value which makes you money whereas, a liability is something which costs you money or causes expenditure.

A detailed list of the most standard assets and liabilities is set out in the example below.

It is essential that you have command of the above information so you can fully begin to understand the true picture of your financial landscape.

Once you have got this information together then the next step is to use the information to get yourself financially organised.

Under this heading you also need to thoroughly check what you are doing with the assets you do have. We will talk more about this later, but for example, are you getting the best rate on your savings account? Are you taking advantage of a tax free ISA? Are you paying too much interest on your mortgage, credit cards or loans, can you consolidate?

Completing these two exercises will give you a true picture of your current financial position, and more importantly make clear the task you face as you proceed through the rest of this book.

Before we move on I want you to pause, and take some time out to carry out the two exercises. The exercises are very important and should not be rushed.

Before going further make a comprehensive list of both your income/expenditure and assets/liabilities on the following pages which have been left blank for this purpose.

Please make your lists as comprehensive as possible; do not leave anything out, not the slightest thing.

FINANCIAL AUDIT

INCOME & EXPENDITURE

Fig1. Monthly Income

INCOME	£
Salary	
Child Benefit	
Interest on savings	
Second/Part Time Job	
Pension	

Once you have your final income figure you need to move on to look at your expenditure on a daily, weekly and monthly basis.

Fig2. Daily Spending Record

EXPENDITURE	
Item	£
Breakfast	
Water/Drinks	
Petrol	
Newspapers/Magazines	
Lunch	
Newspapers	

Fig 3 Weekly Spending Record

Item	£
Groceries	
Spending Allowance	
Restaurant meals include tips	
Kids school expenses	
Hairdressers/Barbers	
Petrol	
Fast Food	
Total of Week	£

Fig4. Monthly Expenditure

Item	Week 1	Week 2	Week 3	Week 4
Groceries				
Restaurant				
Allowance				
Petrol				
Hairdressers				
Mortgage				
Loan				
Credit Card				

The above schedules are just examples and do will obviously have to be tailored to suit your particular circumstances.

Now you have fully identified your expenditure, you need to set it against your income. If your income is on a weekly basis you will need to create a weekly schedule, but since most income is received monthly proceed on this basis, creating your own personal cash flow statement.

Once you have concluded these exercises you will have a much clearer picture of your financial state and be in a position to create your budget, we will discuss this in chapter 3.

www.gototheant.co.uk

NOTES

NOTES

"Did you know that Ants are one of the most organised insects on the planet?

CHAPTER 2

GET ORGANISED!!

Now you have a clearer picture of your financial position it is time for you to get organised and put the information you have acquired to use.

Most people will, once they have completed the above exercise, find themselves falling into one of three groups.

a. **You break even** – your salary and expenditure are about the same so for instance you earn £1500 and your expenditure comes out to approximately £1500

b. Your expenditure exceeds your income so that you effectively make ends meet by **living on an overdraft, credit zone or credit cards.**

c. You have a **little cash left over each month**, but you have credit card debt and perhaps a loan, with a mortgage.

Most of us fall into the **break even category**, living from salary to salary, saving nothing for the future, saddled with debt – in this case you are living on the edge – the financial edge.

This is a serious position to be in, and you should be concerned if you are here because you are totally unprepared for anything unexpected. What if something major happens such as the roof needs repairing or you need to replace your car? The answer is that you probably have no idea how to pay for it unless you put it on the credit card, extend your bank overdraft, credit zone or do something else which is pushing you further into debt!

If you are in the next category (**living on credit**) then you urgently need to take steps to deal with your situation as you are already in debt and living beyond your means. Loss of a job or an extended period of illness without an income could leave you in dire straits financially.

The final category (**little left over**) puts you in a slightly better position than the above two but, still leaves you needing to organize your finances to avoid falling into one of the two other categories and into debt.

Debt

As you will have grasped by now, the major result of the above **income/expenditure** and **asset/Liability** exercises will be to identify our arch enemy on the road to financial efficiency, debt!!

Put simply, you are in debt when you owe more money than you have. Therefore, when your income is exceeded by your expenditure you are running your personal finance on a deficit and are in debt.

Uncontrolled Debt is the enemy of efficient money management and your financial future. I say uncontrolled, because an element of debt is inevitable for most people, for example the most major acquisition you will probably make in your lifetime is your house or flat which will be done with the assistance of a mortgage.

Also, some debt, handled in a disciplined manner can actually be useful; a classic example is the person who utilizes the interest free period on their credit card by paying it off in full every month thereby allowing them to have interest free purchases for anything up to 42 days (See chapter 6 on Financial Education later). Notice I stress **discipline;** if you are reading this book and already have a large unpaid bill on your credit card this is clearly not a suggestion for you.

However, as a principle, debt erodes disposable income which in turn reduces your ability to accumulate savings and thereby reduces your ability to invest and accumulate, and effectively determine the efficient management of your finances.

So it should be clearly stated that **debt is your nemesis**, your number one enemy. So if that's the case, the next step in your journey towards the goal of effective money management must be to have a game plan to get out of debt. Over the remainder of this book you will learn the practical steps you can take in formulating and executing a plan to eliminate debt, take control of your money and create a platform for financial stability by:

Creating your budget,

Stopping the Leaks,

Developing a debt reduction plan,

Becoming financially educated or savvy,

Creating a platform for wealth.

www.gototheant.co.uk

NOTES

_____

_____

_____

_____

_____

_____

_____

_____

_____

_____

_____

_____

_____

_____

NOTES

Did you know that Ants work in teams to move extremely heavy things?

CHAPTER 3

GET TO WORK!!!

Let's make no mistake about it getting your finances under control and developing a plan to effectively manage them is not easy, in fact it is going to be hard work and will require application, dedication and commitment. Remember it took you a while to get into this position so you will need to get to work right away and keep going at it until you are out. So you need to tool up!!!!

A. Budget

Probably the most effective money management tool is a budget. This is using the financial information you have gleaned from your income/expenditure exercise to create a system to help you manage the use of your money efficiently on a daily, weekly, and monthly basis thereby taking control of your finances.

If you have made a comprehensive income/expenditure list in the first exercise in chapter 1 above as instructed, then you are already half way there.

The sole purpose of your budget is to enable you to organize your finances in such a way that you can control your expenditure, thereby ensuring that it does not exceed your income.

As we have already mentioned when your expenditure exceeds your income you are in debt; it will not surprise you to know that the majority of people who live in the United Kingdom today are living in debt; depending on credit cards, overdrafts, and credit zones, which simply mask their true financial condition and delays the eventual day when they have to manage without them, as has increasingly been the case since the onset of the "credit crunch".

A recent report from the Serious Personal Debt Working Group (SPDWG) report paints a chilling picture of the level of personal debt in the UK, which now stands at £1.38 trillion, the equivalent to an average debt per household of £54,452, twice the level of Continental Europe. This is triple the level of 30 years ago. A staggering 7-9 million people in Britain confess to having had a serious debt problem.

Your budget therefore must now become your guide or map on your road to financial freedom and you have to tailor your financial expenditure to strictly comply with it.

Put bluntly, you will have to take every step necessary to ensure your expenditure matches, and does not exceed your income. Until you are back on the road to financial recovery, you will need to distinguish between what you **want** and what you **need**. It is what you need that goes in your budget. So you're going to have to block the leaks (see below).

I know this may sound an almost obvious statement but, in devising your budget you need to pay attention to your money and treat it with respect.

So many people treat money as if it's not important! I know that sounds like a crazy statement but it's true! "I don't have that much so what's the point in paying it any attention? Why should I budget, open a savings account what have I got?

Wrong!!! Your money, no matter what the amount, is not inactive and it will, along with your potential wealth, either accumulate or dissipate depending on the amount of attention you do or do not give it.

Pay your money attention; if you ignore your money, someone else is paying it attention!

Have you noticed how retailers pay attention to even the smallest amount of change in your pockets; they are busy snapping them up with prices like £4.76, £3.85, £2.99, and £1.45; why they don't dismiss your pennies? Retailers know that the old saying "pennies make pounds" is true, especially when it comes to increasing their profit margins. Yet still, how many times have you told yourself "once I break a tenner there is nothing of it left"; well that's clearly not what retailers, supermarkets and the like think, they treat the last penny in your pocket with respect even if you don't.

There is another old saying "take care of the pennies and the pounds will take care of themselves" Your budget will show just how many pennies, and by implication, how many pounds you are wasting. So it is essential that you monitor your budget on a daily, weekly, and monthly basis (yes daily) to track and control your expenditure.

One of the great current financial gurus of our time, and someone I would recommend to you is Martin Lewis; yes Martin Lewis that excitable man on GMTV. Why? Because Martin Lewis stresses the fundamental principle of money management; paying attention to detail and it is only when you begin to pay attention to your money, i.e. where it comes from and where it's going that you can take control of your finances.

So now you need to go to work. Do you know where your money is going?

Before you proceed further take some time out to prepare your budget. As before, you will find a typical budget on the next two pages which you can use as a template. Use the information from daily, weekly and monthly expenditure sheets you prepared earlier to enable you to collate your monthly budget.

I cannot stress enough how important this exercise is, so again, please take your time and ensure you do it thoroughly.

Fig.1 BUDGET

INCOME	Date	£	
Salary 1		£	
Salary 2		£	
Misc Income		£	
Child benefit			£
EXPENDITURE			
Mortgage		£	
Credit Cards		£	
Loans		£	
Overdraft		£	
Gas		£	
Electricity		£	
Water		£	
Telephone		£	
Mobile Telephone		£	
House Insurance		£	
Car Insurance			
Petrol			
Charitable giving			
Allowance			
Saving			

Finished? Good, now let's move on.

Your budget's effectiveness as a tool of money management is wholly dependent on the information you enter into it. I have already stressed above the need to be thorough in relation to your money; and reaffirming this is our next exercise; blocking the leaks!!

B. Blocking the leaks

Imagine a dripping tap, each drip insignificant by itself but, imagine it's dripping on to a wooden floor, slowly but surely the constant flow of water wets, soaks and then permeates the surface weakening it, then rotting it until eventually, whenever the slightest pressure is applied, it simply gives way and collapses.

This is the state of a disorganised financial life. The drips represent the leaks in your finances and the floor represents your financial future. The more you waste your finances by failing to stop the leaks the more you are weakening your financial future.

What are the leakages?

These are the daily, weekly or monthly items of expenditure you don't notice, you don't cater for, they slip under your radar and are doing untold damages to your finances

- Nails
- Car Wash
- Lunch/takeaways/coffee
- Newspapers
- Snacks

• Impulse purchases

Incidental, yet regular purchases as we go about our day to day activities that are the drip drip of financial leakages. You need to remember that everything must go in the budget!

Now imagine the same dripping tap, each little drip still insignificant in itself but, place a container under the tap and leave it for a few minutes, an hour, then a day, a week or a month. Slowly but surely the level of water in the container starts to rise until it's full. That's how an effective savings plan can boost your finances and create a platform for your wealth; but more about that later.

Moving on. Now you have fully ascertained your financial position you need to set about bringing your spending under control, and reducing your debt through the use of your budget.

www.gototheant.co.uk

NOTES

Did you know the Ant **can carry 10 to 20 times its body weight, which is equivalent to a human being lifting a car?**

CHAPTER 4

DEBT CONTROL

If you find you have been spending more that you earn then, as we have already said above you are in debt, and you will now have to make some tough choices:

What can you do without or reduce?

The reality is, depending on your actual circumstances, you may need to undergo a period of austerity when you set about reducing your spending, stopping those leaks, and refine your budget so you look at your daily, weekly and monthly spending to see where you can make cut backs.

What can you sell?

Do you have assets or things you do not need which could be a potential source of income? There is now an ever increasing market for the disposal of unwanted items which can raise additional income. EBay, car boot sales, and the classified sections in the local papers are a few of the ways you can sell unwanted goods. Again, I suggest you make a list of all your assets and then split them into two; one for things you need and the other for those you do not.

You may think that such an exercise is a waste of time, however, the reality is that any money you can raise, no matter how small, that you can put towards tackling your debt and thereby getting your money management scheme on the road as quickly as possible is worth it.

Can you find a secondary income?

To put yourself on a platform where you can benefit from the techniques in this book, you may need to seek short-term additional employment to supplement your income. It is not the purpose of this book to provide you with advice on how you should obtain secondary employment but, it should be noted that the recent growth in the areas of network marketing and internet businesses do provide a host of opportunities for secondary income. There are also the more obvious routes to getting a secondary income such as overtime, a second or part time job or letting a room in your home ;do not rule anything out.

Do you need to get help or professional advice?

If you really are struggling you should consider seeking professional advice. You can get this from a number of organizations; the Citizens advice bureau or Credit Action being two. These organizations will offer advice and assistance in dealing with debt and in some cases actually try and negotiate arrangements with your creditors if you find yourself in serious trouble. There is nothing to be ashamed of or embarrassed about in approaching these organizations, at least your trying to help yourself.

A word to the wise here; beware of rogue so called "debt management companies" offering to mediate with your lenders to get your debts written off for a fee. In many of the cases creditors will not negotiate with such companies and you may actually end up having paid a fee and still have your debts outstanding. There are some legitimate organizations which can assist you in negotiating with your creditors but you need to make sure you fully understand what service the company is actually offering, and how much it is charging, before you commit yourself.

Do you have a debt reduction plan?

In addition to all the above you need to have a plan which deals specifically with you getting out of debt. The reason for this is that most people struggle with trying to pay off a number of debts all at once and simply get nowhere, almost like a revolving door.

My suggestion is the rapid debt replacement plan. There are many different versions of this plan; however put simply this is devising a system of prioritizing payment of your debts based on financial information, and continuing to transfer funds from payment of one debt to another until your debts are completely paid off.

The advantage of the system is that it enables you to set up a plan for reducing your debt in accordance with a clearly defined strategy, and if you follow it through you can end up debt free quicker than you think.

So let's look at how the plan works. Again we will use the information we have gathered from our two previous exercises (income/expenditure and budget) to set out our plan.

Needless to say once again, the plan requires discipline and application but also information of your debts. So here goes:

- List your debts in a schedule including your mortgage, credit cards, loans and overdrafts, credit zone, hire purchase and any other long term financial liability.

- Identify the debt with the highest balance (or rate of interest – you can choose whichever you think suits your circumstances best) because this is the one that will be costing you the most in terms of repayments (or interest) and thereby draining your income.

- Reduce the payments on all your other debts to the minimum amount required and concentrate any spare resources you have on this particular debt.

- Once that particular debt is paid off redirect the amount which you previously used for that monthly payment to the next largest debt until that is paid off. You will now have an amount equivalent to the monthly installment on your two largest debts to transfer onto payments of your next debt and so on until you have paid off all of your debts in full.

As we have said already, you won't clear your debt overnight because you didn't create it over night. What a good rapid debt replacement plan will do is quickly show you how you can bring your debt under control, and begin to release some of your income which was being consumed by your haphazard attempts to pay all of your debts off at once.

Once you have got rid of your debt, and if you are prudent this can happen between 2 and 5 years (depending on the extent of your debt), you can apply the same principle to the payment of your mortgage and clear that off much quicker than the standard 25 years.

Allied to your plan has to be some basic principles of good financial management and this is what we will discuss in the next chapter.

Again, before we move on, take some time to look at the rapid debt repayment schedule as set out on the next page. This is something you can start right now and begin to practically control your debt.

RAPID DEBT REPAYMENT ILLUSTRATION

Fig.1 Original debt payments

Debt	Amount outstanding £	Monthly Payment	Additional Payment
Credit Card (2)	£ 2,750.00	£110.00	
Credit Card (1)	£ 4,500.00	£140.00	
Loan	£10,000.00	£230.00	
Overdraft	£ 450.00	£ 35.00	
Hire Purchase	£ 1,300.00	£ 90.00	
Debit Card	£ 2,000.00	£ 100.00	

Fig.2 Debt payments using rapid debt repayment scheme

Debt	Amount	Monthly Payment (Min Payments)	Additional Payment
Loan	£10,000.00	£230.00	**£110.00**
Credit Card (1)	£ 4,500.00	£100.00	£40.00
Credit Card (2)	£ 2,750.00	£ 80.00	£30.00
Debit Card	£ 2,000.00	£ 80.00	£20.00
Hire Purchase	£ 1,300.00	£ 70.00	£20.00
Overdraft	£ 450.00	£ 35.00	-

- Take the debt with the highest monthly amount payable: Loan

- Reduce payments on all other outgoings (except your mortgage of course) to minimum payments this leaves you with a surplus of £110.00

- Divert the excess funds to monthly payment of the loan so you are now paying £340.00 thereby reducing the principal debt, and monthly interest and clearing the balance much more quickly.

- Continue until the loan is completely paid off and then move on to the next highest interest paying debt which is credit card (1).

- Maintain this pattern throughout all your debts with the twofold result of lowering your debt and freeing up income.

The obvious advantage, as already stated is that you will eliminate debt quicker thereby reducing your monthly outgoings and creating a new pool of income which can be used.

www.gototheant.co.uk

NOTES

Did you know that Ants have two stomachs, one for eating and one for storing food?

CHAPTER 5

MANAGE YOUR MONEY

"It's not how much you make but how much of it you actually keep" (Wayne Malcolm)

Now you have embarked on your debt reduction plan, you must also begin to manage your money effectively, in other words make it work for you.

The ultimate aim of financial management is to enable you to create a financial surplus which you can then use to build a platform, first for savings, then investment and finally for the creation of wealth and your own financial independence.

Your budget will have identified the areas of recurring expenditure; loans, credit cards, groceries and utility bills. Your rapid debt reduction plan will have now begun to bring your debt under control.

However, the next step is to actually begin, like the Ant, to become proactive rather than reactive and prepare financially for every possible call there may be on your financial resources. You are now moving on to one of the most important steps in developing your financial strategy, which is managing the surplus funds for which up to now; there has been no defined purpose.

Your money management plan

Not surprisingly, you again need a plan. Not another one, I hear you moan, yes, another one. It is the lack of a plan or an organised system of managing your money that has or will get you into a financial mess, and trust me; it is a plan that will get you out. Before we get on to the plan lets establish a fundamental principle upon which to base our plan:

One of the golden rules of financial management is **"always pay yourself first!**

This is for two reasons:

Firstly, if you spend everything you make on bills and have nothing left at the end of the month you are not making progress, and will find yourself back in exactly the same position the following month, this is dangerous because (as we have said before) all it takes is one month's missed salary, redundancy, or a long term illness to wreck all the hard work you have done to get to this point.

Secondly, how will you prepare without any savings or surplus funds for that unexpected emergency; new washing machine, a new item of furniture, an unexpected trip abroad to see an ill relative, or even a holiday? The reality is that some or nearly all of these things will happen to you at one time or another. One of the main reasons for financial mismanagement is the failure to prepare for an emergency, when this happens; our best laid financial plans are completely disrupted.

The answer is to find a way to use your surplus funds, and like the Ant store them for the above events. How do you do this, by creative accounting of course.

And how do we do this? By creating a plan to streamline and diversify our income into a number of different accounts.

Multiple accounts

So now you have your income and you need a debt-proof plan that has a formula:

Remember, the first leg of this is to pay your debts in accordance with your debt repayment plan, so it becomes clear almost immediately that you need to split your income.

So if you have a monthly salary of say a £1000 per month and £700 - £800 per month is being allocated towards your rapid debt repayment plan then that still leaves £200 - 300 per month for you to manage.

That £300 represents your payment to yourself and how you manage this is as crucial to your financial future as your debt repayment plan. There are a number of ways in which you need to allocate this portion of your income which is fundamental to your plan.

The most efficient way of proceeding is to create a number of different accounts each of which have a different purpose. Clearly, you do not need to physically set up a different bank account for each fund you create but it would be helpful. You can use a spreadsheet to manage the channeling of your income into different funds as long as you maintain the discipline to actually carry out the exercise.

Here are the recommended funds for you to set up:

- **Living Fund** - you will need to allocate a percentage for you daily living expenses (see income/expenditure schedule and your budget). It is essential that you use the information you have already acquired from the above exercises to accurately forecast how much you really need as you don't want to be dipping into your other accounts if you find you can't survive on the amount you have allocated yourself in your living fund. **The best place for this particular fund is your current account which is accessible on a daily basis.**

- **Emergency Fund** – you need to allocate a percentage of your income towards a short term savings plan for emergencies. This fund is to deal with minor emergencies such as car repairs, your washing machine breaking down, and emergency bills. This account stops you reverting back to using your credit cards or overdraft in the event of an emergency, and messing up your rapid debt repayment plan.

- The best place for this fund would be a deposit account which is easily accessible but, not so much so that you can pull it out for an impulse purchase. Such an account will also offer a better rate of interest than a current account. **NB:** An emergency is not a new sofa or holiday; these should be planned for.

- **Contingency Fund** – A contingency fund is a pool of money which has a specific purpose, such as to replace your income during seasons of unemployment or to bridge the gap in the event of a major financial emergency – this fund should ideally have a sum in it equivalent to at least 6 months' of your salary. Your contingency fund should be in an account that pays a competitive rate of interest. Such an account will probably require you to give notice before withdrawal.

- **Freedom fund** - The freedom fund is for such things as the title suggests, a dream holiday, once in a life time cruise, retirement bungalow, home abroad, something you have always dreamt of.

- **Long term saving account.** – Is for your investing money which you are using for your long term plans such as retirement. It should not be touched and should be in an account which offers the best rate of interest, and is not easily accessible such as an ISA Account, National Savings Certificate or a Bond. This kind of account should run alongside your pension.

To assist you in understanding the multiple account concept I have prepared a diagram setting out how it works. This is just an illustration so you don't have to set yours up in exactly the same way. You may for example amalgamate your contingency and emergency account or your long term savings and dream account thereby reducing the number of accounts you have to maintain. The underlying principle, however, is that you streamline your income so it's apportioned to the various priorities set out above.

www.gototheant.co.uk

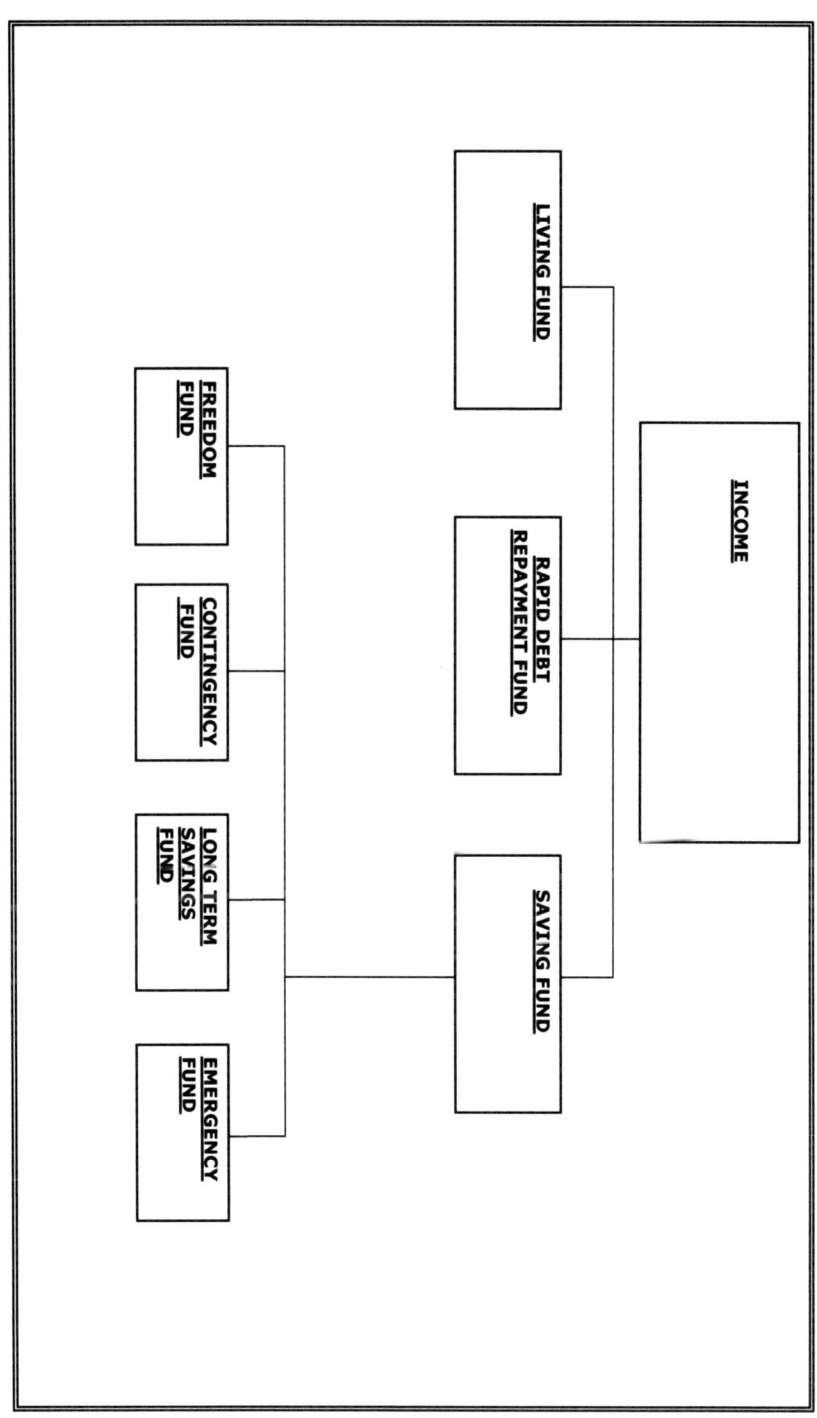

NOTES

"Did you know the **Ant's brain is the largest amongst insects?**
It has been estimated that an ant's brain may have the same
processing power as a Macintosh II computer.

CHAPTER 6

FINANCIAL EDUCATION

Equally important as the practical steps we have
considered so far in this book is your personal financial
education. If you are going to get out of debt, stay
out of debt, take control of your finances, and create
a platform for wealth you need to develop and
increase your financial education. I deal with sources
of financial information and literature in the next
chapter but, in this chapter we need to look at ways
of increasing your financial education.

Poor money management and the resulting debt are
created through financial ignorance. The reality is that
despite money being the most important thing, most
people spend very little time acquiring knowledge of
how to manage it.

A recent report by **Data monitor**, a market research
analyst, makes chilling reading; it found that:

- UK borrowers account for one third of
  unsecured debt in western Europe

- On average, a Briton has twice the debt of a European

- Total consumer debt in the UK is at a record £1.3 trillion

- New debt last year came to an unprecedented £215bn

- Citizens Advice faced 1.25 million new debt cases last year and the figure is rising

The Report goes on to say

Britain's "buy now, pay later" consumer culture has led to unprecedented levels of personal debt. The average Briton now has more than twice as much unsecured borrowing - including overdrafts, personal loans and credit card debt - as the typical European.

The market research analysts state that even before mortgage borrowing was considered, the average Briton owes £3,175, compared to the average debt in Europe of £1,588. Data monitor said Britons had "an insatiable appetite for credit", taking on new unsecured loans of £215bn last year alone.

Frightening isn't it?

So you need to get educated about how money works so all the decisions you make in the future are made intelligently.

Savings – "A part of all you earn is yours to keep" (George Clason)

A 2009 study by Yorkshire Building Society has shown that if the average Briton lost their job, they would only be able to survive on their savings for 52 days. But more worryingly, the results suggest that over a third (36 per cent) only have access to £500 worth of savings, which translates to just 11 days' survival. The study states:

"In the current economic climate, this research paints an extremely alarming picture for those consumers without any protection products in place. Finances for many are already finely balanced due to the rising cost of living and research reveals that both state benefits and savings are not viable options for the majority of consumers to rely upon for an adequate length of time."

According to the study, the average level of savings currently stands at £2,474, while average outgoings are £1,445 per month.

From the above you can see that a savings plan is fundamental to any money management strategy. Just how important saving is to your plan is exemplified by the **Rule of 72**

This rule basically states that in order to find the number of years required to double your money at a given interest rate; you divide the compound return into 72. The result is the approximate number of years that it will take for your investment to double. For example, if you want to know how long it will take to double your money at 12% interest, divide 12 into 72 and you get six years (72 months).

In essence, the value of your money saved doubles every six years and the higher the rate you invest at the quicker you can double your investment. So if you invest at 10% and over you can double your return in 6 years. Now, obviously at the current interest rates you are unlikely to be able to find risk free investments with that kind of return, but it is the principle I want you to understand.

Under your management plan you will have various savings accounts, however, you need to ensure that the accounts you use provide the best return on your money and is fit for its purpose.

Whilst it is not the purpose of this book to provide advice with regards to specific accounts; as a basic foundation for your savings plan you should generally look for:

Individual Savings Plan – These allow you to save up to £7,200 per year in a combination of shares and cash accounts **tax free**. Whilst cash ISA accounts can be gauged on the basis of the interest rates paid on the account, this is not the same with an investment stocks and shares ISA, and accordingly funds should only be invested in these types of accounts after careful professional advice – These are for long term savings.

Bonds – These are accounts which offer a fixed term return over a specific period of time such as 1, 3 or 5 years. These types of accounts are very secure and ideally should not to be touched during the fixed term. You obtain a higher return if you leave it for full term. This type of account would be useful for your freedom and investment funds.

Notice Accounts – As the name suggests these are accounts under which you are required to give notice before making withdrawals; usually 60-90 days and again reward you with a higher rate of return depending on infrequent withdrawals Contingency Accounts.

Basic Savings Account – usually instant withdrawal accounts with very low interest rates but good for emergency accounts.

INVESTMENTS

Stocks, Shares, Equities, Currencies, Commodities Property Investment

This is a very complex area and beyond the scope of this book, although hopefully one day your financial management techniques will take you to the place where you can invest at this level. For now the one piece of advice I would give you on these types of investments is that they should only be entered into with specialist advice from a qualified Independent Financial Adviser.

CREDIT - *"Credit is like a rope. You can use it as a tool or tie it into a noose to hang yourself" (Mary Hunt)*

Earlier I touched on the subject of credit and said I would return to it. As this is a book regarding financial management and debt reduction the widespread use of credit is not something I recommend, however, I am realistic enough to appreciate that there may be circumstances in which the use of credit is necessary, and if disciplined may actually be useful. So let's look at the most common forms of credit.

Credit cards–After several reckless episodes I personally do not have a credit card and recommend that only those of you with the best financial discipline make one a part of your financial tool kit. Credit Cards are one of the main sources of debt in the United Kingdom today.

Despite all the bad press credit cards are not all bad news when used as a tool for money management. What credit cards should never be used as is a substitute for income or to purchase goods when you have run out of money and clearly have no means of repaying.

On the positive side, a credit card can be a useful tool if you can pay it off every month and use the extended period (potentially up to 42 days) to assist your money management strategy.

Of fundamental importance in choosing a credit card, or any form of credit for that matter, is the interest you will pay if you do not clear it entirely every month. You must ensure that you obtain a competitive rate and ascertain from the outset what the APR (the annual percentage rate) is. See below for an explanation of APR.

Also remember on a credit card you can in some cases be charged up to three different rates of interest:

- rate for **purchase** of goods- this is usually the standard rate for the card.

- rate for **balance transfers** (see below) – can vary depending on the deal you have been offered; can be as low as 0% in the initial transfer period but will rise to the standard rate once this has finished.

- rate for **cash withdrawals** – this is usually the highest and interest is charged immediately the cash is withdrawn with no interest free period

There are some cards which offer an initial 0% rate for an introductory period or a balance transfer facility whereby a debt from a card with a higher rate of interest to another card with a lower; sometimes up to 8 months. These can, if used properly be a useful way of reducing interest payment on high rate cards but again considerable discipline is required to take advantage of such a facility and to avoid ending up with a number of cards after the offers have expired with even higher rate interest on them.

Buy now pay later – this type of credit again offers you an initial interest free period when you can take the goods (car, furniture etc) without payment, and after that period is complete you either pay one lump sum (inclusive of the rounded up interest) or effectively enter into a loan agreement. Again, whilst there are certain advantages to this it has its drawback, and ends up pushing you back into credit. Why not save the 12 months instead and then purchase the goods outright yourself without credit (freedom fund).

Again, in the event you decide to go down that road you need to check the APR on any agreement you are entering, and think carefully about whether you are able to commit to such a long term commitment.

Again, my advice is not to use this type of credit unless you are an extremely disciplined person. You should, if you are serious about financial management be using your freedom fund to take care of such emergencies.

Loans – The same principle as set out above applies to loans. Avoid them if you can but, if you must use them look around for a competitive rate.

Loans are not all bad either. As mentioned earlier, consolidation loans are often used as a means of bringing a number of debts under one financial commitment, and this is recognised as a valid debt reduction strategy. As will be obvious, this is not necessarily a strategy that this book advocates and caution needs to be exercised to ensure that you do not end up in a worse position than you were originally.

Notwithstanding the above, there may be occasions on which you may simply have no option but to go down this route. One point to consider is trying to obtain a loan which can be paid off early with no redemption penalties.

I personally do not recommend loans for the purposes of buying cars, furniture, going on holidays, planning and paying for weddings. These are things that should be paid for through a disciplined savings plan rather than resorting to credit.

Money Smart

As we have said before you need to be money smart and although I deal with sources of financial information in the next chapter I would like to take time out to recommend a particular website that can assist in this regard. This website www.moneysavingexpert. com/tips   has many tips on how you can save money on loans, credit cards, insurance etc. The site is run by Martin Lewis.

I have a few money smart tips myself which are as follows:

- Earlier we discussed the APR in relation to credit transactions. This is important as it shows how your total debt is calculated and how much extra you stand to repay on the amount you have borrowed. The APR is the rate that is charged to you by a bank (or any other financial institution) on the amount you have borrowed over a one year period. The rate includes simple interest on the principal amount borrowed, plus other fees and charges. This then translates into an APR. For example if you borrowed £2000 for one year and the interest and other fees total £360, the APR would be 18%, or 1.5% monthly (1.5% x 12 months = 18%)

- The rule of 72 applies for your debt also; your interest charge can double over 6 years also depending on how high your interest charge is.

- To get a good return of interest you must shop around.

- Make sure that you never take out the loan for the full term; so if you take out a five year loan at £150 per month make sure you can pay more each month so the loan ends before the 5 years. The longer you take to pay the loan the more interest you will owe.

- Make sure that you take out a loan, or a mortgage for that matter, which allows for early redemption, otherwise you may find you have to pay a penalty for paying your loan off early.

- Always pay your bills on time. I know this sounds basic but arrears on cards, overdrafts and loans attract interest, and on other bills may even end up in court fines, which in turn may end up damaging your credit rating.

- Where possible always use direct debits or standing orders they provide certainty for you as to when payments are leaving your account and also guarantee payment to your creditors

- If you are already in a critical situation with debts and are facing possible court proceedings or bankruptcy seriously consider a consolidation loan, this option however needs to be very carefully thought through. More on this later.

- When buying a car do not buy a brand new one as a car is a depreciating asset, which means the minute you take it off the forecourt , that car looses value, up to two or three thousand. You can buy a car which has been in the show room for a year it will have very little mileage and save you a few thousand pounds.

- Better still, get a second hand car with just one owner let someone else take the depreciation.

- An important part of your Management Plan should be to have financial security for your family in the event that you should die. A Life Insurance plan is therefore essential. Detailed advice on such policies is again beyond the scope of this book but there are numerous companies that provide this service and a cursory glance at the website should point you in the direction of a qualified IFA Advisor who can provide you with the information you need.

- Equally important is your pension for a part of your post retirement income. Most companies run a pension scheme for their employees, if your company does, you should ensure you join up right away and if your company does not run one you should arrange to take out your own private one as soon as possible. It is a fact that pension schemes, which largely derive their income and growth from the stock markets, have been severely hit by the credit crunch; however, it is still important that you keep this long term part of your plan fully up to date. Again you should consult an IFA about which type of pension is best for you.

A word of warning! Once you become financially astute and begin to manage your finances you will find that you suddenly have a lot of new friends. Your Bank manager, who previously never had any time for you (apart from threatening to close your account), will now be plying you with offers of a loan, new credit card, extended overdraft or credit zone facilities.

Not just your bank manager but also credit card companies, loan companies; everyone is going to want a part of the new you and unless you are disciplined and stick to the financial principles which you have learnt in this book, you are going to end up right back where you started in debt and out of control financially.

Not everyone is going to like you getting out of debt and making sensible choices about how and where you spend your money but that's just tough because you are in this for the long haul; this is the beginning of your new financial journey and you are not going back.

www.gototheant.co.uk

NOTES

NOTES

Did you know the Ant can adapt to any catastrophe within the colony by changing its duties to deal with the situation?

CHAPTER 7
FINANCIAL MINDSET

Action/Attitude

The purpose of developing your financial education is to ensure that your attitude towards financial matters, as well as your actions, undergoes a complete change. Reading all the books in the world on finances, including this one, will be of no use unless you have a fundamental change of mind about how you are going to manage your money.

Now let's be real for a minute it is going to be hard so don't expect to be perfect immediately. You will have acquired your bad financial habits over many years so don't beat yourself up if it doesn't all go right immediately. If you fall simply get up and try again.

A good exercise to help you with developing your new financial mindset is to motivate yourself with the potential benefits of your financial management strategy:

Better lifestyle,

Freedom from debt,

Platform for wealth.

Another fundamental key to developing your new financial mindset is obviously changing what goes into your mind. It's time to put down the glossy magazines and start reading the finance section of the Times on a weekend, time to put down the novels and start reading more books like this one that can teach you money management principles, it's time to turn off the television soaps for a little while and start watching the Money Programme or listening to the Money Box on Radio 4. In other words it's time to get serious about your finances.

By now you should have worked out this book is not a Get Rich Quick book or a Seven Steps to becoming a Millionaire publication, however, I should make it clear that I have nothing against such books which deal with wealth creation; indeed, I read a large number of those books myself prior to writing this one; however before you can get to that stage it is essential that you do the ground work of getting your finances in order and thereby building a platform for creating real wealth and true financial independence.

So, as can be seen, on your journey to financial development it is important that you consolidate the progress you have made by expanding your financial intelligence. There are a multitude of financial publications and websites that you can gain access to which can assist you in this regard.

As I have previously said one of my favourite web sites is www.moneysavingsexpert.com run by Martin Lewis who has also published a number of books on the ways in which you can manage your money effectively.

I would also recommend the following publications:

1. The Rules of Wealth by Richard Templar

2. The Richest Man in Babylon by George Clason

3. The Millionaire next Door by Thomas J Stanley

4. Think and Grow Rich by Napoleon Hill

5. Creating your Personal Money Map by Ethan Pope

6. Rich Dad Poor Dad by Robert T Kiosaki

7. From Trash Man to Cash Man by Myron Golden

8. Money for Life by Alvin Hall

These publications will help you develop a wider understanding of personal finance matters and money management techniques.

There are also a number of useful organisations which I refer to throughout this book who can also assist you on your financial management journey:

1. Credit Action –
   www.creditaction.org.uk

2. Citizens Advice Bureau –
   www.citizensadvice.org.uk

3. MoneyStuff.co.uk –
   www.moneystuff.co.uk

4. Consumer Credit Counselling Service –
   www.cccs.co.uk

5. Association of Independent Financial Advisers –
   www.aifa,net/consumer-area

6. Independent Financial Advice –
   www.unbiased.co.uk

7. Financial Services Authority –
   www.fas.gov.uk

www.gototheant.co.uk

NOTES

NOTES

The main purpose of the Ant is to collect food for the hive

CHAPTER 8

A PLATFORM FOR WEALTH

Hopefully you should now have in place a system for managing your finance; that is identifying your assets and liabilities, income and outgoings. With your budget, debt repayment plan and your multiple accounts should now mean that you are in full control, in theory anyway, of your finances.

As we said, the most immediate benefit of your plan is that you will have expendable income which you will channel into your various accounts. The primary aim of this exercise is to enable you to provide a financial buffer of security but, it does not yet provide you with the financial independence that you require.

As I made clear at the outset this is a ground level book for you to commence your financial management journey. It can be used by anyone earning any amount at any stage of their financial progression; all it requires is a commitment from you to turn your finances around.

Hopefully what this book does is bring you to a place where you can begin to look at longer term, complex and possibly higher risk investment, in other words a platform for wealth. This should be your ultimate aim so that you are prepared for any financial eventuality.

I know this may seem a way off now but it is not as far-fetched as it seems. In the publication "The Millionaire Next Door" the author Thomas J Stanley gives numerous examples of ordinary Americans who have become millionaires simply by using basic money management techniques similar to those set out in this book and the other publications referred to in chapter 7 above. So the next question is if they can why can't you?

The Ant collects more than enough for the colony so you need to save more than enough for your future.

www.gototheant.co.uk

NOTES

NOTES

Did you know the Ant that the average lifespan of the Ant is 45-60 days making it one of the most productive insects during its short lifetime

CHAPTER 9

CONCLUSION

We started with the Ant so let's finish with it and look at some of its attributes that will greatly assist you on your journey to financial wholeness:

1. **It prepares for winter while it is summer** - Do not wait until the next "credit crunch" to get your finances in shape sort them out now. As I said in the introduction, the economic cycle means that sooner or later the economic outlook will brighten, and you need to be in a position to take advantage of this and prepare for the next downturn.

2. **Its eyes are on the future** – You can't change your financial past but you can and must take steps to deal with your financial future. The steps in this book will help you take those steps but, only if you are willing to make the difficult decisions for your long term financial future.

3. **It has the ability to delay gratification** – If you don't have the patience to wait and curb your expenditure while you are developing your strategy you will mess up your financial future. The Ant takes the resources it collects in the summer and moves it towards winter. Will somebody else show up to do it for the Ant? No! Are there predators looking for an opportunity to steal what the Ant has got? Yes, but it's so focussed it doesn't have time to worry about where it is.

4. **It has a cause bigger than itself** – The Ant regularly takes on and tries to move food which is considerably larger than itself; it is not just providing for itself but also for members of its colony. The financial decisions you make are often not only for you but also your spouse, members of your family or your business. When you make your decisions always keep in mind the bigger picture.

Finally, I cannot complete this book without making mention of my wife Pauline Carter for whom a large amount of the credit for this book should go to. For years as the "man of the house" I insisted that I should be responsible for the management of our financial affairs. Of course I never had a plan or a budget and simply adopted the good old fashioned method of attempting to pay all the bills at the same time in a haphazard fashion.

I steadfastly refused to use standing orders or direct debits and had credit cards, debit cards, loans and overdrafts. The result was a total disaster and meant

I never had any savings or money for an emergency, which basically meant I was constantly in debt.

This book therefore is born out of my own personal experience and I can testify that adopting the Ant's principles does indeed work. I am now turning from the Ant into the squirrel storing and saving up nuts to provide a Platform for Wealth, but this my friend is the subject of another book.

I sincerely hope that this book has helped you in developing a financial management system and turning your finances around so that at the onset of the next financial winter you will, like the Ant, be prepared.

www.gototheant.co.uk

ASPIRE TO INSPIRE BEFORE YOU EXPIRE

Unknown............

Lightning Source UK Ltd.
Milton Keynes UK
11 April 2011

170713UK00001B/35/P